For the Teacher

This reproducible study guide to use in conjunction with a specific novel, consists of lessons for guided reading. Written in chapter-by-chapter format, the guide contains a synopsis, pre-reading activities, vocabulary and comprehension exercises, as well as extension activities to be used as follow-up to the novel.

In a homogeneous classroom, whole class instruction with one title is appropriate. In a heterogeneous classroom, reading groups should be formed: each group works on a different novel on its reading level. Depending upon the length of time devoted to reading in the classroom, each novel, with its guide and accompanying lessons, may be completed in three to six weeks.

Begin using NOVEL-TIES for reading development by distributing the novel and a folder to each child. Distribute duplicated pages of the study guide for students to place in their folders. After examining the cover and glancing through the book, students can participate in several pre-reading activities. Vocabulary questions should be considered prior to reading a chapter; all other work should be done after the chapter has been read. Comprehension questions can be answered orally or in writing. The classroom teacher should determine the amount of work to be assigned, always keeping in mind that readers must be nurtured and that the ultimate goal is encouraging students' love of reading.

The benefits of using NOVEL-TIES are numerous. Students read good literature in the original, rather than in abridged or edited form. The good reading habits, formed by practice in focusing on interpretive comprehension and literary techniques, will be transferred to the books students read independently. Passive readers become active, avid readers.

SYNOPSIS

A Day No Pigs Would Die is the semi-autobiographical account of Robert Newton Peck's coming of age in rural Vermont as well as a tribute to his father, Haven Peck, who was a farmer and pig slaughterer.

The story begins with an energetic narrative of Robert's struggle to deliver the calves of Apron, his neighbor's cow. Before the incident is over, he has delivered one of the cow's twin calves, ripped a ball-size goiter from her throat, and has had his arm gnawed and torn by the angry new mother. Robert's determination to act as a midwife to Apron pays off handsomely when her owner, Benjamin Tanner, gives Robert a pet piglet, Pinky, as payment for his services to the cow.

Robert's father Haven entertains thoughts of keeping Pinky from eventual slaughter as a brood sow if she can produce a farrow of piglets each year. But when Pinky proves to be barren, Haven and Robert try hard to ignore the inevitable task of having to slaughter her.

When Haven is unable to trap a deer with which to feed his family over the winter, he is forced by necessity to kill Pinky for her meat. At the moment when Pinky's blood splatters the snow, Robert experiences a storm of emotions: he hates his father for killing his pet even as he understands she must be killed. Seeing tears in Haven's eyes, Robert's heart fills with love for his father as he understands how hard it is for him to do his duty no matter how much it hurts.

One autumn day Haven tells his son: ". . . This is my last winter. . . . You got to face up to it. You can't be a boy about it." Very quietly, on the third day in May, Haven Peck dies in his sleep. At the age of thirteen, Robert has to step into the void created by Haven's death. He must assume the responsibilities of burying his father, running the farm, and providing for his family.

On the day Robert buries the hardworking and honest man who was his father, he realizes that everything has changed. Haven Peck, silenced by death, can no longer do his job; the very rhythm of life has been disrupted for this is the day that no pigs would die.

AUTHOR INFORMATION

Robert Newton Peck III was born on February 17, 1928 in Vermont. He was raised by his parents, Haven and Lucille Peck, to appreciate the virtues of hard work and honesty. Indeed, *A Day No Pigs Would Die* is a tribute to his father.

Peck received his baccalaureate degree from Rollins College in 1953 at the age of twenty-five. From 1945 to 1947 he served as an infantryman in the U.S. Army. He then spent several years writing television commercials and jingles—catchy songs promoting particular products—for New York advertising agencies.

Peck's first book was *A Day No Pigs Would Die*. He was influenced by his relationship with his father, an illiterate farmer and pig slaughterer, whose wisdom contributed to Peck's understanding of the natural order of life. Peck is an accomplished writer who tends to base his stories on people and places that he has known, adding embellishment for artistic purposes. This is true of *A Day No Pigs Would Die*, a story which is true-to-life in its attention to detail and the spirit of truth, but which does not recount real events as they actually happened. Peck may have woven the thread of Shakerism throughout this book to explain his character's philosophy of work as worship, even though he was not a Shaker.

In 1958, Peck married Dorothy Anne Houston. They have two children: a daughter, Anne Houston, and a son, Christopher Haven. Peck devotes most of his time to writing works of juvenile fiction, many of which are based on historical events that took place in New England. Like his father, he is also a farmer. Each February he acts as director of the Rollins College Writers Conference, a position he has held since 1978. He is a prolific writer who produces at least four books a year.

PRE-READING DISCUSSION QUESTIONS AND ACTIVITIES

1. Bring into class photographs of rural homes, farms, and country towns, or anything else that will help you and your classmates visualize farm life. Use the photographs as the basis for a mural or collage to place on the bulletin board.

2. What is a county fair? Try to find pictures and newspaper articles about a county fair. What are some of the events that typically occur at such a fair? What kinds of displays are shown?

3. Robert Newton Peck, the author of *A Day No Pigs Would Die*, has written a semi-autobiographical novel. How does a biography differ from an autobiography? What do you think a semi-autobiography might be? Read the Author Information on page two of this study guide. As you read the book, try to figure out what parts of the book might be based on the author's life and what parts might be fiction.

4. Read the dedication at the beginning of the book. What kind of relationship do you think the author had with his father? As you read, determine whether Peck captured the personality of the man he described in the dedication.

5. Have you ever felt temporary hatred for someone you loved? What made you feel that way? How long did it last?

6. Can you remember a time when you or someone you know had to perform a seemingly terrible act out of love for another person? What happened afterwards? What happened to the relationship with the other person?

7. Make a list of the chores that you do at home. Compare the kinds of chores that would be required in a city apartment, a suburban home, and a small country farm. Do you think parents should require their children to do jobs around the house on a regular basis? Do you think that you are asked to do more than your fair share? How much work can a parent require before it would seem to be exploitation?

8. Here are examples of proverbs, or wise sayings, that are still spoken:
    - Haste makes waste.
    - Waste not, want not.
    - A bird in the hand is worth two in the bush.
    - A stitch in time saves nine.

    Are there any proverbs that are used frequently in your family?

CHAPTERS 1 - 3

Vocabulary: Draw a line from each word on the left to its definition on the right.
Then use the numbered words to fill in the blanks in the sentences below.

1. provoke

2. fret

3. goiter

4. ridge

5. debt

a. enlargement of the thyroid gland, usually on the front and side of the neck

b. something that is owed; an obligation to pay

c. anger; stir up feelings or emotions

d. narrow elevation of land; chain of hills or mountains

e. feel or express worry

. . . .

1. Standing on the _____, we could see our little town nestled down in the valley.

2. The _____ had become so large that it was choking the cow.

3. It is better to prepare for a hurricane, rather than just stand around and _____.

4. I felt a great sense of relief once all my _____ was paid.

5. Samantha knew her black eye would _____ lots of questions from her classmates.

Questions:

1. Why was Robert determined to help Apron?
2. Why did Robert beat Apron at the same time that he was trying to help her?
3. How was Robert's arm injured?
4. What kind of relationship did Robert have with his family? Provide examples from the story to support your opinion.
5. What did Haven Peck do for a living? Would you prefer to meet him during the week or on Sunday? Explain.
6. According to Haven, how did fences create peace, and not war, among all creatures in nature? Do you agree with him?

Chapters 1 - 3 (cont.)

7. Why was Robert surprised to see Apron with two calves?
8. Why did Haven at first refuse the pig? Why did he change his mind, allowing Robert to accept the gift?

Questions for Discussion:

1. How was Robert's way of life different from that of most children in Learning? How does it compare with your way of life? Do you think children should have to abide by their parents' ways even if it makes them the victims of their peers' teasing?
2. Why do you think the author described the birth of the calf, sparing none of its graphic details? Do you think the episode would have been better or worse without the details?
3. Do you think Haven Peck was an intelligent man? What kind of knowledge did he share with his son?

Language Study: Colloquialism

A colloquialism is an expression which is usually accepted in informal writing or speaking but not in a formal situation. Indicate what each of the underlined colloquialisms means in the following sentences.

1. Instead of <u>tying into him</u> . . .

   _____

2. I was going to <u>light into</u> Edward . . .

   _____

3. I don't <u>cotton to</u> raise a fool.

   _____

4. I <u>owe you a sorry</u> for being so late.

   _____

5. I'd <u>turned a tail</u> and run off . . .

   _____

Chapters 1 - 3 (cont.)

Literary Devices:

I. *Point of View* — In literature, point of view refers to the voice that is telling the story. The author may choose to narrate the story as an objective voice. This is called a third person narrative. Or he may choose to have one of the characters in the story narrate. This is called a first person narrative.

What is the point of view in this novel?

_____

How does this point of view affect the language of the story and the events that take place?

_____

_____

_____

_____

_____

II. *Characterization* — In the first page of the novel, the boy reveals a great deal about himself. Find the words that provide evidence for the following conclusions:

- He has had little formal schooling
- He does not dress like the other boys.
- He is proud of the way he lives even if others make fun of him.

Math Connection:

If a "stone" equals 14 lbs., how many lbs. will Pinky weigh as an adult pig if it grows to 300 stone?

Writing Activity:

Write about a time when you had to endure a physically painful experience as Robert had done. Unlike Robert, were you given anything to dull the pain? Were you as brave as Robert? Describe the experience and your reactions to it.

CHAPTERS 4, 5

Vocabulary: The numbered words refer to farmyard animals, kinds of farm enclosures, and farm equipment. Draw a line from each word on the left to its definition on the right. Then place each numbered word in its best category below.

1. capstan
2. tack room
3. yoke
4. corn cratch
5. bay
6. Holstein
7. sty

a. pen for swine
b. breed of black and white dairy cattle
c. crib to hold fodder
d. reddish-brown horse
e. rotating handle used to wind cable or rope
f. room near the stable used to store saddles
g. harness in the form of a crosspiece with two bow-shaped pieces to enclose the heads of two animals

Animals	Enclosures	Farm Equipment

Questions:

1. What descriptive phrases did the author use to make the reader feel affection for the pig?

2. Why was it unusual to name a pig on the Pecks' farm?

3. What evidence revealed that Robert was an extremely intelligent boy even though his language was unsophisticated and his father was illiterate?

4. How had society made Haven Peck a second-class citizen? Why did he claim this was unfair? Do you agree with Haven?

5. What did Haven mean when he compared himself to those who were not Shakers, saying "I am rich and they are poor"?

6. How did families like the Pecks spend Sunday?

7. In what ways did Pinky behave like a pet?

8. What was Haven and Robert's attitude toward work?

Chapters 4, 5 (cont.)

Questions for Discussion:

1. How did the playthings that the author remembered from his youth, such as the whistle made from bark and the flutterwheel, differ from those that children use today?
2. Do you think it is wise for Robert to become so attached to Pinky?

Art Connection:

Draw a diagram of Robert's flutterwheel based on the description in Chapter Five. Use arrows to show how the wheel would turn and label all the parts.

Social Studies Connection:

Find a map of Vermont and its surrounding states. Locate the places mentioned in the book: Rutland and Learning in Vermont; Ticonderoga and Lake George in New York State.

Writing Activity:

Imagine that Robert had a friend in another town to whom he wanted to write about Pinky. Write such a letter as if you were Robert, describing Pinky and your growing feelings toward the pig.

CHAPTERS 6 - 8

Vocabulary I: Use the context to figure out the meaning of the underlined word in each of the sentences below. Circle the letter of the word or phrase you choose.

1. The doctor had an ointment for every ache and pain and a <u>remedy</u> for every illness.
    a. relief   b. cure   c. medicine   d. diagnosis

2. Noticing the teacher sigh and wipe her brow, I knew that teaching me grammar was a <u>tribulation</u>.
    a. joyous occasion   b. feast   c. worry   d. business

3. The hawk buried his <u>talons</u> in the rabbit's fur and whipped it through the juniper bush.
    a. feathers   b. wings   c. beak   d. claws

4. After not eating a meal in twelve hours, my stomach felt <u>vacant</u>.
    a. queasy   b. full   c. empty   d. heavy

Vocabulary II: The male, female, and offspring of an animal species may have different names. Use a dictionary to help you place the words from the Word Box in the appropriate places in the chart below.

WORD BOX

boar	cow	mare
bull	gander	piglet
calf	goose	sow
colt	gosling	stallion

Species	Male	Female	Offspring
1. swine			
2. cattle			
3. goose			
4. horse			

Chapters 6 - 8 (cont.)

Questions:

1. How did the author make the reader aware of the passage of time?
2. Why was Robert amused when he learned that Aunt Matty would be his tutor?
3. Why was Robert frightened when he learned that his tutor, Aunt Matty, was a Baptist?
4. What did Aunt Matty mean when she said, "Next time I'll teach the pig"?
5. What kind of special care did Robert give Pinky?
6. What plans did Robert have for Pinky's future?
7. Why did Haven bring his gun on the night he took Robert to the graveyard?
8. How did Haven show that he approved of Sebring's action?

Question for Discussion:

Why do you think Robert did well in every subject except English?

Literary Devices:

I. *Simile* — A simile is a figure of speech in which two unlike objects are compared using the words "like" or "as." For example:

> I could see the red of his [a hawk's] tail—like a torch against the softer colors of his underbody.

What is being compared?

_____

What is the effect of this comparison?

_____
_____

Find another example of a simile. Give the page number and tell what is being compared.

_____
_____
_____

Chapters 6 - 8 (cont.)

II. *Personification* — Personification in literature is a figure of speech in which the author grants human qualities to nonhuman objects. For example:

> It [wild paintbrush] didn't seem to want to mix with the clover, and it just kept to its own kind.

What is being personified?

_____

How does this help you visualize the scene?

_____

_____

_____

Reading as Story Theater:

Chapter Six, when Aunt Matty becomes a tutor for Robert, is an excellent vehicle for story theater. One student can read the narrative text, and two others can read the dialogue for Aunt Matty and Robert. Find simple props, such as two side chairs, several bracelets, and a handkerchief. Rehearse reading the chapter aloud before you read it to your class.

Writing Activity:

Imagine that you are Robert Peck writing a journal entry about the previous night's events. Describe what you overheard in the kitchen, what you witnessed at the graveyard, and how you felt about Sebring Hillman returning with the child's coffin.

CHAPTERS 9, 10

Vocabulary: Many words in English have multiple meanings. Consider the several definitions for each of the following words. Circle the letter of the definition that best fits the way the word is used in the sentence below. Then choose one of the other definitions and use the word in an original sentence.

brace

    a. support; fortify

    b. pair

    c. clamp or clasp

1.   A brace of oxen pulled the tractor across the field.

    _____

sound

    a. in good condition; free from injury

    b. noise

    c. measure the depths of water

2.   If you want a sound body, you should eat healthy foods and exercise several times a week.

    _____

stock

    a. shares of a particular company

    b. goods or merchandise

    c. ancestry or descent of a group of related animals

3.   We expect that pig to have fine offspring because she comes from a long line of excellent stock.

    _____

shed

    a. structure built for storage

    b. pour forth, as a fountain

    c. drop out, as hair

4.   A poodle is one of the few breeds of dog that does not shed.

    _____

Chapters 9, 10 (cont.)

Questions:

1. What does Robert's encounter with Ira Long at the widow Bascom's house reveal about the hired hand and his relationship with the widow?
2. Why was Robert excited about going to the Rutland Fair?
3. Was Rutland a great city or did it just appear so to Robert? Explain.
4. Why did Robert think it might be sinful to enjoy exhibiting the yoke of oxen?
5. What happened to the ten cents Aunt Carrie gave Robert to enjoy at the fair?
6. What did Robert mean when he said at the end of Chapter Ten that "the merry-go-round went a whole lot faster, and I'd fall off for certain"?

Questions for Discussion:

Haven Peck was a man of few words but he expected a high standard of behavior from his son. How did Haven expect his son to behave among adults? What advice have you received from adults about how you should behave?

Art Activity:

Draw a picture depicting Robert in the ring with Pinky when she received her medal.

Writing Activities:

1. Imagine you are Robert and write a letter home telling about your day at the fair. Describe your feelings as well as the events themselves.
2. Write about a time when you visited a place that made you as excited as Robert was when he went to the fair in Rutland. Describe your feelings prior to the visit, the visit itself, and finally, whether the experience lived up to your expectations.

CHAPTERS 11, 12

Vocabulary: Read the definitions below and then tell what the same word means in a different context.

1. If <u>barren</u> land is acreage that produces no plants or trees, what is a <u>barren</u> animal?

   _____

   _____

2. If <u>lean</u> meat is devoid of fat, what is a <u>lean</u> crop?

   _____

   _____

3. If to <u>fester</u> means to putrefy or rot, what is an idea that <u>festers</u>?

   _____

   _____

4. If a <u>chamber</u> is an enclosed space, what might the <u>chamber</u> of a gun hold?

   _____

   _____

Questions:

1. Why did Haven think he was doing Ira Long a favor by allowing his dog to confront the weasel?

2. What bitter lesson did Robert and his father learn when they weaseled Hussy?

3. Why was it important for Pinky to have offspring?

4. What lesson about nature did Robert learn when he observed the hens eating the squirrel meat?

5. What evidence revealed that Robert's values sometimes conflicted with those of his family?

Chapters 11, 12 (cont.)

Questions for Discussion:

1. How would you assess the way Haven Peck faced his approaching death?

2. Why do you think Haven did not permit any physical affection to accompany his serious conversation with his son?

3. Do you think Haven should have been so forthright with Robert or should he have protected him more against the tragedy of his oncoming death?

Literary Devices:

I. *Symbolism* — In literature a symbol is an object, an event, or a character that represents an idea or a set of ideas. Read the following passage from Chapter Twelve and tell what the fire symbolized:

> I sat watching the red cinders turn gray. I stayed there until the fire had died. So it would not have to die alone.

_____

_____

Do you think that this is an effective symbol? Explain.

_____

_____

II. *Foreshadowing* — Foreshadowing is a literary device in which the author provides clues to events that will occur later in the novel. What were the many ways that the author foreshadowed Haven Peck's announcement to his son that he was dying?

_____

_____

_____

_____

Writing Activity:

Write about a time when you received some serious news that would affect your life. Tell how the news was conveyed and your reactions to the information.

CHAPTERS 13 - 15

Vocabulary: Analogies are equations in which the first pair of words has the same relationship as the second pair of words. For example, DAY is to NIGHT as UP is to DOWN. Both pairs of words are opposites. Complete the following word analogies from the choices below.

1. THRESHOLD is to LINTEL as BOTTOM is to _____.
    a. opposite   b. parallel   c. top   d. surface

2. URBAN is to RURAL as DULL is to _____.
    a. suburban   b. stupid   c. free   d. keen

3. WEDDING is to JOYOUS as FUNERAL is to _____.
    a. somber   b. burial   c. content   d. bored

4. SCISSORS is to PAPER as _____ is to GRASS.
    a. hammer   b. seed   c. scythe   d. tractor

5. REVEILLE is to MORNING as _____ is to EVENING.
    a. vespers   b. bells   c. prayers   d. dinner

Questions:

1. What comment was Robert making about his father when he said, "he's been trying all his life to catch up to something. But whatever it is, it's always ahead of him, and he can't reach it"?

2. Why did Robert's life and future success on the farm take on new meaning?

3. What was the significance of Robert kissing his father's hand? What evidence showed that Haven Peck appreciated his son's gesture?

4. How did Robert behave on the day of his father's death? What did this reveal about his character?

5. Why did Robert concentrate on his father's tools on the day of the funeral? What did they symbolize to him?

6. What did the attempted signatures in the cigar box reveal to Robert about his father?

7. Explain the Pecks' attitude toward death as epitomized in the statement: "They came to help us plant Haven Peck into the earth."

Chapters 13 - 15 (cont.)

Questions for Discussion:

1. Do you think Mr. Tanner really knew or had suspicions about Haven Peck's poor health when he was having a discussion with Robert? If so, do you think he should have been more forthright?

2. Why do you think Haven did not offer Robert explanation or consolation on the morning they killed Pinky? Do you think this was the right way to handle the situation? Do you think Robert should have attended the killing?

3. Why do you think the author described Pinky's death in such bloody detail?

4. Do you think the Peck family treated Haven's death in a manner that was consistent with their usual behavior? Do you think you could treat the death of a loved one in a similar manner?

Writing Activity:

Imagine that you are a friend of the Peck family and you have been called upon to speak at Haven Peck's funeral. Write a eulogy for him and say some of the things that Robert might have said.

CLOZE ACTIVITY

The following excerpt is taken from the beginning of Chapter Seven. Read the entire passage. Then fill in each blank with a word that makes sense. Afterwards, you may compare your language with that of the author.

Up on the ridge north from our house, it was open field. You could walk for

most _____[1] a mile before reaching the woods.

The _____[2] was high now. And seeing as I'd _____[3]

all day on the hay wagon with _____,[4] it sure felt good just to know

_____[5] evening chores were done, and I could _____[6] on my

back in the soft grass _____[7] do nothing except wait for evening.

Pinky _____[8] with me, and she was lying down _____.[9]

Even though she hadn't put in a _____[10] of work all day. But there she

_____,[11] a mound of white pig in a _____[12] field of purple

clover and kickweed. Here _____[13] there was a stand of wild paintbrush.

_____[14] of yellow, and some red. It _____[15] seem to want to mix

with _____[16] clover, and it just kept to its _____[17] kind.

The whole hillside was purple clover; _____[18] in the early sundown,

it looked more _____[19] than I'd ever see it. Pinky was _____[20]

in it. Over and back, over and _____.[21] I knew it felt good to her,

_____[22] I was lying in it myself, and _____[23] clover felt right and

good to me. The clover was getting ripe now, and you could take a big red-purple ball

of it in your hand, and pull out the flower shoots.

FRAMED PARAGRAPH

Read the entire passage before you go back and fill in the blanks with appropriate information. When you are finished, you will have a summary of the story.

A Day No Pigs Would Die is a semi-autobiographical novel about the childhood of the author, _____. Most of the book concerns the relationship between Robert and _____, and Robert and _____. Each of these relationships bring both joy and tragedy.

The wonderful pig that Robert has raised since infancy made Robert feel proud when _____
_____.

But when it was discovered that Pinky was barren, _____
_____
_____.

On that day Robert felt _____
_____
_____.

Although Haven Peck was just a poor pig slaughterer, he was loved and revered by his son. Robert respected his father because _____
_____
_____.

In order to prepare for his imminent death, Haven _____
_____
_____.

At the end of the novel it was clear that Robert had grown up. He showed his maturity by _____
_____
_____.

Robert's legacy from his father was _____ -
_____
_____.

POST-READING DISCUSSION QUESTIONS AND ACTIVITIES

1. The plot in literature refers to the events that occur in sequence. In many stories the events are ordered so that there is a pattern of *rising action* that culminates in a *climax*, or turning point, followed by events of *falling action*, ending in a *resolution*. Using a diagram such as the one below, note the main events that constitute the rising action, the turning point, and the falling action. Then briefly explain the resolution.

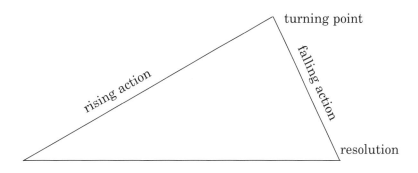

2. With your classmates, discuss how Robert changed during the course of the novel, and the factors that brought about these changes. Then discuss how his parents remained unchanged and the lasting values they represented.

3. The setting of a work of fiction refers to the place and time where the story occurs. Discuss the importance of setting in this novel, and how the characters have been shaped by their setting.

4. **Literary Element:** Themes are central ideas, often not directly expressed, that provide the foundation for a story. Find supportive evidence within the text for the following themes:
    - Work is sacred and each job, no matter how lowly, must be respected and executed well.
    - Wealth is defined by love of family and love for the earth, rather than by riches.
    - Being an adult means meeting adversity with strength.
    - The passage from childhood to adulthood is difficult.

5. Most societies have rites of passage for their young as they are initiated into adulthood. Within the framework of the novel *A Day No Pigs Would Die*, how was Robert initiated into adulthood? Was it through an established ritual? Was it violent?

7. There are very few scenes in which the characters actually display their emotions through words or elaborate actions, yet this story is full of details which hint at the emotions underlying the words. List the incidents in which emotions surface. Then list the situations in which emotions are not explicitly expressed. Why do you think the author chose to understate most of the emotional experiences in the book?

Post-Reading Discussion Questions and Activities (cont.)

7. This novel explores life by contrasting it with death. Discuss the many death scenes in this book. Describe each incident, and tell what each scene represents.
   - The hawk swoops from the sky and kills a rabbit.
   - Sebring Hillman digs up the grave of his child.
   - The dog and weasel battle violently inside a barrel, and the weasel is killed. The dog is so seriously wounded that it must be killed out of mercy.
   - Robert kills a squirrel for its undigested nutmeats.
   - Haven slaughters Pinky.
   - Haven dies.

8. In this book, Robert Newton Peck depicts the cycle of life lived close to nature. Significantly, the book begins with a violent, bloody birth, and ends with a calm, peaceful death. Tell why you think the author chose to structure the book in this way. Why do you think the author had Haven become ill in winter? Why did Haven die in the spring?

9. The passage of time was closely linked to the events in this novel. In a chart, tell the major events that occurred during each season. Why do you think the author had Haven become ill in winter? Why did Haven die in the spring?

10. **Literature Circle:** Have a literature circle discussion in which you tell your personal reactions to *A Day No Pigs Would Die*. Here are some questions and sentence starters to help your literature circle begin a discussion:
    - How are you like Robert? How are you different?
    - Do you find the characters in the novel realistic? Why or why not?
    - Who else would you like to read this novel?
    - What questions would you like to ask the author about this novel?
    - It was not fair when . . .
    - I would have liked to see . . .
    - I wonder . . .
    - Robert learned that . . .

SUGGESTIONS FOR FURTHER READING

Cleaver, Bill, and Vera Cleaver. *Trial Valley*. HarperCollins.

* _____. *Where the Lilies Bloom*. HarperCollins.

* Cushman, Karen. *Catherine, Called Birdy*. HarperCollins.

Fox, Paula. *A Place Apart*. Farrar, Straus & Giroux.

Greene, Bette. *Beat the Turtle Drum*. Random House.

Harlan, Elizabeth. *Footfalls*. Simon & Shcuster.

* Holman, Felice. *Slake's Limbo*. Simon & Schuster.

* Paterson, Katherine. *Come Sing Jimmy Jo*. HarperCollins.

Peck, Richard. *Father Figure*. New American Library.

* Rawlings, Marjorie. *The Yearling*. Simon & Schuster.

* Rawls, Wilson. *Where the Red Fern Grows*. Random House.

Reader, Dennis. *Coming Back Alive*. Random House.

Sebestyen, Ouida. *Far From Home*. Little, Brown.

* Spinelli, Jerry. *Maniac Magee*. HarperCollins.

* Steinbeck, John. *Of Mice and Men*. Penguin.

* Taylor, Mildred D. *Roll of Thunder, Hear My Cry*. Penguin.

* _____. *The Pearl*. Penguin.

* Voigt, Cynthia. *Dicey's Song*. Simon & Schuster.

* _____. *Homecoming*. Simon & Schuster.

Other Books by Robert Newton Peck

Banjo. Random House.

Basket Case. Random House.

Clunie. Random House.

Eagle Fur. Random House.

Fawn: A Novel. Little, Brown.

Kirk's Law. Random House.

Soup. Random House.

Trig. Random House.

* NOVEL-TIES Study Guides are available for these titles.

ANSWER KEY

Chapters 1-3

Vocabulary: 1. c 2. e 3. a 4. d 5. b; 1. ridge 2. goiter 3. fret 4. debt 5. provoke

Questions: 1. Robert was determined to help Apron because he was ashamed of running away from trouble in the past when he was teased by his peers at school. 2. Robert beat Apron because he was frustrated that the calf was not being born, and he wanted the cow to move forward so that the pants leg tied around the calf's head would pull the calf from its mother's womb. 3. When Robert stuck his arm into the cow's mouth to remove the goiter, she bit down hard; thus injuring Robert. 4. Robert had a warm, loving relationship with his family. Answers to the second part of the question may vary, but should mention that Robert trusted his mother to sew up his arm, and that his father showed tenderness at his son's bedside during his recovery. 5. Haven Peck was a slaughterer of pigs. It would be best to meet him on Sunday when he did not reek of pigs' blood. 6. According to Haven, fences allowed people to know what was theirs and what belonged to their neighbors. There would be no disputes about boundaries, and consequently, there would be peace between neighbors. Answers to the second part of the question will vary. 7. Robert was surprised to see Apron with the calves because he didn't know he had helped Apron deliver twin bull calves. 8. At first Haven refused the pig because he did not think Robert should be paid for doing something that was expected of him. He only accepted the gift on behalf of his son when Mr. Tanner said it could be payment for future work that Haven Peck would do for him.

Colloquialisms: 1. tying into him – scolding him severely 2. light into – fight with 3. cotton to – want to; prefer to 4. owe you a sorry – owe you an apology 5. turned a tail – turned around

Chapters 4, 5

Vocabulary: 1. e 2. f 3. g 4. c 5. d 6. b 7. a; Animals — bay, holstein; Enclosures — corn cratch, tack room, sty; Farm equipment — capstan, yoke

Questions: 1. The author used descriptive phrases such as "little pink nose," "rubbing against my boots . . . like a cat," "prettiest piglet," to make the reader feel affection for the pig. 2. Pigs were a business and meant to be slaughtered, not have names like house pets. 3. Robert was intellectually curious, consulting books to find the answers to questions. He received high marks in school, showing on tests that his knowledge was broader than that which the test required. 4. Society had made Haven a second-class citizen because he was illiterate and could not vote. He thought it was unfair to equate intelligence with the ability to read and write: it did not take into account his practical knowledge. Answers to the second part of the question will vary. 5. Haven felt that his family was rich in its strong family ties, and because of the land they tended, which would soon belong to them outright. 6. Sunday was spent at Meeting, a religious service. 7. Like a pet, Pinky would go for walks with Robert and would never wander far away. She would come to Robert for solace if she were frightened. 8. Haven and Robert believed that work was their mission. Any task, no matter how menial, had to be taken seriously and executed carefully.

Chapters 6-8

Vocabulary I: 1. b 2. c 3. d 4. c

Vocabulary II:

Species	Male	Female	Offspring
1. swine	boar	sow	piglet
2. cattle	bull	cow	calf
3. goose	gander	goose	gosling
4. horse	stallion	mare	colt

Questions: 1. Robert, as narrator, revealed the months that passed as he commented on the weather, life on the farm, and Pinky's development. 2. Robert was amused because he confused the word "tutor" with "tooter," and thought Aunt Matty was going to teach him the cornet. 3. Robert had heard about baptism and was afraid Aunt Matty, as a Baptist, would immerse him in water. 4. Aunt Matty made her disparaging remark after concluding that Robert was too stupid to learn her grammar lesson. 5. Robert fed Pinky table food, gave her fresh milk, wet down her straw, built her a special sty, and played with her. 6. Robert did not want Pinky to be slaughtered for food. Instead, he planned that Pinky would be a fine brood sow who would be mated with Mr. Tanner's pig Samson. 7. Haven brought his gun because he thought he might have to use force to stop Sebring Hillman from digging up the grave. 8. Haven showed his approval by putting aside his gun and allowing Hillman to return to his wagon, carrying the coffin of his illegitimate child to be buried on Hillman land.

Chapters 9, 10
Vocabulary: 1. b 2. a 3. c 4. c
Questions: 1. Answers will vary, but should include the idea that Ira Long was a kind, thoughtful man despite public gossip. This man had caused Mrs. Bascom to change from a dour widow to a joyful woman. 2. Robert was excited because he had never been away from home before and had never been exposed to anything as exciting as a county fair. 3. Robert thought Rutland was exciting because he had never been to a city before, not even a small one like Rutland. 4. Robert worried that showing the yoke of oxen might be interpreted as showing pride, something that his family thought was sinful. 5. With the ten cents Aunt Carrie had given him, Robert paid for soap to clean Pinky after the pig had rolled in manure. 6. Robert was describing his dizziness prior to fainting in the pigs' exhibition ring.

Chapters 11, 12
Vocabulary: 1. A barren animal cannot have offspring. 2. A lean crop is sparse; does not produce much food. 3. An idea festers when it is evil and stays in your thoughts, making you gloomy and anxious. 4. Ammunition is held in the chamber of a gun.
Questions: 1. Haven thought the dog would survive the battle and would thereafter hate weasels and protect the Bascoms' chicken coop. 2. Robert and Haven learned that they had contributed to a brutal and unnatural conflict. This should never have been allowed, even if it meant that all of their hens might ultimately succumb to weasels. 3. If Pinky could have offspring, she would not have to be slaughtered for profit. The Pecks could not afford to keep unproductive animals. 4. Robert learned that life was sometimes unfair with the greater rewards going to the stronger creatures. 5. Robert wanted a coat that could be bought in a store even though the quality might be inferior to his mother's manufacture, and his parents could not afford its purchase. He also envied those who were able to buy material things.

Chapters 13-15
Vocabulary: 1. c 2. d 3. a 4. c 5. a
Questions: 1. Robert meant that his father had been striving for undefined, unreachable goals. 2. Robert's future success on the farm took on new meaning because his father was dying, his two brothers were dead, and his sisters were married and no longer lived at home. This left Robert as the only "man" to care for his mother and Aunt Carrie and be responsible for paying off the farm for five years. 3. Answers will vary to the first part of the question, but should include the idea that Robert was showing that his hatred for his father had abated and that he had forgiven his father for slaughtering the pig. Robert noticed his father wipe his eyes, suggesting that he had become tearful in response to his son's kisses. 4. On the day of his father's death, Robert did his chores, calmly informed his mother and Aunt Carrie of his father's death, and then went into town to inform the person who officiated at Shaker burials. Robert had clearly matured in his father's image, showing sensitivity, strength, and restraint. 5. Robert concentrated on his father's tools because their worn, beautiful handles symbolized his father's attitude toward work as a mission. 6. The attempted signatures symbolized Haven's futile yearning to better himself by becoming literate. 7. This statement suggested that death was an inevitable part of the cycle of nature, and that life began anew each spring despite the tragedy of death.